WORDS FOR OUR TIME

Susan Kapuscinski Gaylord

susangaylord.com

ISBN 978-0-9891642-3-8

Photos by Kevin Harkins
harkinsphotography.com

Words have always been my ballast and my anchor. I believe in their power. While I understand the saying "actions speak louder than words," I believe that words can be where actions start. Throughout history, words have provided the spark to begin change and the sustenance to carry it through.

Words For Our Time is a series of artworks based on eight words: strength, hope, truth, peace, justice, love, courage, and compassion. Each was created from one large sheet of paper that was torn into separate sections. After the writing was complete, the pieces were sewn back together in an act of healing as I mended the torn paper and made it whole.

There are two ways of exerting one's power: one is pushing down, the other is pulling up.
— Booker T. Washington

When I dare to be powerful, to use my strength in the service of my vision, it becomes less and less important whether I am afraid.
AUDRE LORDE

STRENGTH

Those who contemplate the beauty of the earth find reserves of strength that will endure as long as life lasts.
Rachel Carson

You GAIN STRENGTH, COURAGE, AND CONFIDENCE BY EVERY EXPERIENCE IN WHICH YOU REALLY STOP TO LOOK FEAR IN THE FACE. YOU ARE ABLE TO SAY TO YOURSELF, "I HAVE LIVED THROUGH THIS HORROR. I CAN TAKE THE NEXT THING THAT COMES ALONG. ELEANOR ROOSEVELT

There is no strength to be gained from hurting one another. Only weakness.
— Ursula K. Le Guin

We are only as strong as we are united, as weak as we are divided.
J.K. Rowling

When strength is yoked with justice, where is a mightier pair than they?
Aeschylus

STRENGTH

There are two ways of exerting one's strength: one is pushing down, the other is pushing up.

—BOOKER T. WASHINGTON, THE GREAT QUOTATIONS, EDITED BY GEORGE SELDES, 1960

When I dare to be powerful, to use my strength in the service of my vision, it becomes less and less important whether I am afraid.

—AUDRE LORD, THE CANCER JOURNALS, 1980

Those who contemplate the beauty of the earth find reserves of strength that will endure as long as life lasts.

—RACHEL CARSON, THE SENSE OF WONDER, 1965

You gain strength, courage, and confidence by every experience in which you really stop to look fear in the face. You are able to say to yourself, "I have lived through this horror. I can take the next thing that comes along."

—ELEANOR ROOSEVELT, YOU LEARN BY LIVING, 1960

We are only as strong as we are united, as weak as we are divided.

—J. K. ROWLING, HARRY POTTER AND THE GOBLET OF FIRE, 2000

There is no strength to be gained from hurting one another. Only weakness.

—URSULA K. LE GUIN, THE DISPOSSESSED, 1974

When strength is yoked with justice, where is a mightier pair than they?

—AESCHYLUS, FRAGMENT, 1, 298

HOPE

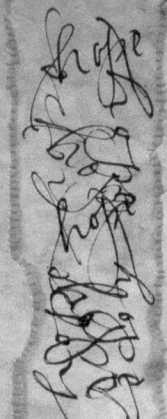

Of hope is forlorn
is for when all
JRR Tolken

If you lose hope, somehow you lose the vitality that keeps life moving, you lose that courage to be, that quality that helps you go on in spite of it all. And so today I still have a dream. Martin Luther King Jr.

HOPE, IN THIS DEEP AND POWERFUL SENSE, IS NOT THE SAME AS JOY THAT THINGS ARE GOING WELL, OR WILLINGNESS TO INVEST IN ENTERPRISES THAT ARE OBVIOUSLY HEADED FOR EARLY SUCCESS, BUT RATHER, AN ABILITY TO WORK FOR SOMETHING BECAUSE IT IS GOOD, NOT JUST BECAUSE IT STANDS A CHANCE TO SUCCEED. HOPE IS DEFINITELY NOT THE SAME THING AS OPTIMISM. VACLAV HAVEL

The hope is always here, always alive but only your fierce caring can fan it into a fire to warm the world. SUSAN COOPER

We must accept finite disappointment, but never lose infinite hope. MARTIN LUTHER KING JR.

to BE HOPEFUL IN BAD TIMES... IS BASED ON THE FACT THAT HUMAN HISTORY IS A HISTORY NOT ONLY OF CRUELTY, BUT ALSO OF COMPASSION, SACRIFICE, COURAGE, KINDNESS. HOWARD ZINN

Hope is a thing with feathers that perches on the soul. Emily Dickinson

HOPE

Oft hope is born when all is forlorn.

—J. R. R. TOLKIEN, THE RETURN OF THE KING, 1955

If you lose hope, somehow you lose the vitality that keeps life moving, you lose that courage to be, that quality that helps you go on in spite of it all. And so today I still have a dream.

—MARTIN LUTHER KING, JR., A CHRISTMAS SERMON ON PEACE, EBENEZER BAPTIST CHURCH, ATLANTA, GA, DECEMBER 24, 1967, PUBLISHED IN A TESTAMENT OF HOPE: ESSENTIAL WRITINGS OF MARTIN LUTHER KING, JR., EDITED BY JAMES MELVIN WASHINGTON, 1986

Hope, in this deep and powerful sense, is not the same as joy that things are going well, or willingness to invest in enterprises that are obviously headed for early success, but, rather, an ability to work for something because it is good, not just because it has a chance to succeed.

—VACLAV HAVEL, DISTURBING THE PEACE, 1990

The hope is always here, always alive, but only your fierce caring can fan it into a fire to warm the world.

—SUSAN COOPER, SILVER ON THE TREE, 1977

We must accept finite disappointment, but never lose infinite hope.

—MARTIN LUTHER KING, JR., THE WORDS OF MARTIN LUTHER KING, JR., EDITED BY CORETTA SCOTT KING, 2002

To be hopeful in bad times is based on the fact that human history is a history not only of cruelty, but also of compassion, sacrifice, courage, kindness.

—HOWARD ZINN, YOU CAN'T BE NEUTRAL ON A MOVING TRAIN, 2002

Hope is a thing with feathers that perches on the soul.

—EMILY DICKINSON, POEM 254, c. 1858–1862

It takes two to speak the truth one to speak and another to hear Thoreau

When a great truth once gets abroad in the world no power on earth can imprison it, or prescribe its limits, or supress it. FREDERICK DOUGLASS

truth truth truth truth truth truth truth truth truth truth truth truth truth truth truth truth

Truth, truth, truth, truth, truth, truth, truth, truth, truth, truth, truth, truth

Truth alone will endure, all the rest will be swept away before the tide of time. Mahatma Gandhi

TRUTH

Rather than love, than money, than fame, give me TRUTH Thoreau

truthtruthtruthtruthtruthtruthtruthtruthtruthtruthtruthtruthtruthtruthtruthtruth

REPETITION DOES NOT TRANSFORM A LIE INTO A TRUTH. FRANKLIN DELANO ROOSEVELT

truth truth truth truth truth truth truth truth truth truth truth truth

...a great nation doesn't shy away from the truth. It strengthens us. It emboldens us. It should fortify. BARACK OBAMA

Facts do not cease to exist because they are ignored. Aldous Huxley

YE SHALL KNOW THE TRUTH, AND THE TRUTH SHALL SET YOU FREE. JOHN 8:31

TRUTH

It takes two to speak the truth—one to speak, and another to listen.

—HENRY DAVID THOREAU, A WEEK ON THE CONCORD AND MERRIMACK RIVERS, 1849

When a great truth gets abroad in the world, no power on earth can imprison it, or prescribe its limits, or suppress it.

—FREDERICK DOUGLASS, SPEECH TO THE INTERNATIONAL COUNCIL OF WOMEN, WASHINGTON, DC, MARCH 31,1888, PUBLISHED IN WOMEN'S JOURNAL, APRIL 14, 1888

Truth alone will endure, all the rest will be swept away before the tides of time.

—MAHATMA GANDHI, BASIC EDUCATION, 1951

Rather than love, than money, than fame, give me truth.

—HENRY DAVID THOREAU, WALDEN, 1854

Repetition does not transform a lie into a truth.

—FRANKLIN DELANO ROOSEVELT, RADIO ADDRESS, OCTOBER 26,1939, REPORTED IN THE BALTIMORE SUN, OCTOBER 27, 1939

... a great nation doesn't shy away from the truth. It strengthens us. It emboldens us. It should fortify.

—BARACK OBAMA, DEDICATION OF THE NATIONAL MUSEUM OF AFRICAN AMERICAN HISTORY AND CULTURE, WASHINGTON, DC, SEPTEMBER 24, 2016

Facts do not cease to exist because they are ignored.

—ALDOUS HUXLEY, COMPLETE ESSAYS 2, 1926–1929

Ye shall know the truth, and the truth shall make you free.

—JOHN 8:31, KING JAMES BIBLE

WE MUST COME TO SEE THAT THE END WE SEEK IS A SOCIETY AT PEACE WITH ITSELF, a SOCIETY THAT CAN LIVE WITH ITS CONSCIENCE.

MARTIN LUTHER KING Jr.

And the world will live as one
JOHN LENNON

When the power of love overcomes the love of power, the world will know peace.

No Sri Chinmoy

FOR it ISN'T ENOUGH TO TALK OF PEACE... AND it ISN'T ENOUGH TO BELIEVE IN it. ONE MUST WORK At IT.

ELEANOR ROOSEVELT

peace PEACE peace PEACE

PEACE

PEACE PEACE PEACE PEACE

Peace cannot be kept by force. It can only be achieved by understanding.

Albert Einstein

True peace is not merely the absence of tension; it is the presence of justice.

Martin Luther King Jr.

Peace peace peace peace peace peace

You can't separate peace from freedom because no one can be at peace unless He has his freedom. Malcolm X

PEACE

We must come to see that the end we seek is a society at peace with itself, a society that can live with its conscience.

—MARTIN LUTHER KING, JR., SPEECH: HOW LONG, NOT LONG, STATE CAPITOL BUILDING, MONTGOMERY, AL, MARCH 25, 1965

And the world will live as one.

—JOHN LENNON, IMAGINE, 1971

When the power of love overcomes the love of power, the world will know peace.

—NO SRI CHINMOY, MY HEART SHALL GIVE A ONENESS FEAST, 1993

For it isn't enough to talk of peace. One must believe it. And it isn't enough to believe in it. One must work at it.

—ELEANOR ROOSEVELT, VOICE OF AMERICA BROADCAST, JANUARY 7, 1944

Peace cannot be kept by force. It can only be achieved by understanding.

—ALBERT EINSTEIN, SPEECH TO NEW HISTORY SOCIETY, NEW YORK, NY, DECEMBER 14, 1930

True peace is not merely the absence of tension; it is the presence of justice.

—MARTIN LUTHER KING, JR., STRIDE TOWARD FREEDOM, 1958

You can't separate peace from freedom because no one can be at peace unless he has his freedom.

—MALCOLM X, SPEECH, NEW YORK, NY, JANUARY 7, 1965

And justice always into mercy grew. *John Greenleaf Whittier*

WE WILL NOT BE SAT-IS-FIED ... UNTIL

Justice is truth in action *Benjamin Disraeli*

INJUSTICE ANYWHERE IS A THREAT TO JUSTICE EVERYWHERE MARTIN LUTHER KING JR

JUSTICE

Justice is a conscience, not a personal conscience but the conscience of the whole of humanity. ALEXANDER SOLZHENITSYN

ROLLS DOWN LIKE WATER AND RIGHT-EOUS-NESS LIKE A MIGHTY STREAM. MARTIN LUTHER KING JR.

The arc of the universe is long but it bends toward justice. MARTIN LUTHER KING, JR.

WHENEVER A SEPARATION IS MADE BETWEEN LIBERTY AND JUSTICE, NEITHER IS IN MY OPINION, SAFE. EDMUND BURKE

JUSTICE

And justice always into mercy grew.

—JOHN GREENLEAF WHITTIER, THE PENNSYLVANIA PILGRIM, 1872

We will not be satisfied ... until justice rolls down like water and righteousness like a mighty stream.

—MARTIN LUTHER KING, JR., SPEECH AT THE MARCH ON WASHINGTON FOR JOBS AND FREEDOM, WASHINGTON, DC, AUGUST 28, 1963

Justice is truth in action.

—BENJAMIN DISRAELI, SPEECH BEFORE THE HOUSE OF COMMONS, LONDON, ENGLAND, FEBRUARY 11, 1851

Injustice anywhere is a threat to justice everywhere.

—MARTIN LUTHER KING, JR., LETTER FROM BIRMINGHAM JAIL, BIRMINGHAM, AL, APRIL 6, 1963

Justice is conscience, not a personal conscience but the conscience of the whole of humanity.

—ALEXANDER SOLZHENITSYN, LETTER TO THREE STUDENTS, OCTOBER, 1967

The arc of the universe is long, but it bends toward justice.

—MARTIN LUTHER KING, JR., BACCALAUREATE SERMON AT WESLEYAN UNIVERSITY, MIDDLETOWN, CT, JUNE 7, 1964

Whenever a separation is made between liberty and justice, neither is, in my opinion, safe.

—EDMUND BURKE, LETTER TO A FRENCH GENTLEMAN, OCTOBER 1789

DARKNESS CANNOT DRIVE OUT DARKNESS. HATE CANNOT DRIVE OUT HATE: ONLY LOVE CAN DO THAT. MARTIN LUTHER KING JR.

Love doesn't just sit there, like a stone, it has to be made, like bread; remade all the time, made new. URSULA K. LE GUIN

LOVE RECOGNIZES NO BARRIERS. IT JUMPS HURDLES, LEAPS FENCES, PENETRATES WALLS TO ARRIVE AT ITS DESTINATION FULL OF HOPE. MAYA ANGELOU

LOVE

where there is hatred, let me sow love. SAINT FRANCIS

love love love love love love love love love love love love

JUST AS LOVE FOR ONE INDIVIDUAL WHICH EXCLUDES THE LOVE OF OTHERS IS NOT LOVE, LOVE FOR ONE'S COUNTRY WHICH IS NOT PART OF ONE'S LOVE FOR HUMANITY IS NOT LOVE BUT IDOLATROUS WORSHIP. erich fromm

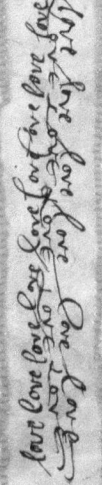

love that conquers hate, peace that rises triumphant over war, and justice that proves more powerful than greed FRED ROGERS

love and compassion are necessities, not luxuries. without them, humanity cannot survive. Tenzin Gyatso 14th Dalai Lama

LOVE

Darkness cannot drive out darkness: only light can do that. Hate cannot drive out hate: only love can do that.

—MARTIN LUTHER KING, JR., STRENGTH TO LOVE, 1963

Love doesn't just sit there, like a stone, it has to be made, like bread; re-made all the time, made new.

—URSULA K. LE GUIN, THE LATHE OF HEAVEN, 1971

Love recognizes no barriers. It jumps hurdles, leaps fences, penetrates walls to arrive at its destination full of hope.

—MAYA ANGELOU, FACEBOOK, JANUARY 11, 2013

Where there is hatred, let me sow love.

—SAINT FRANCIS OF ASSISI, PRAYER OF SAINT FRANCIS

Just as love for one individual which excludes the love for others is not love, love for one's country which is not part of love for humanity is not love, but idolatrous worship.

—ERICH FROMM, THE SANE SOCIETY, 1955

Love that conquers hate, peace that rises triumphant over war, and justice that proves more powerful than greed.

—FRED ROGERS, COMMENCEMENT ADDRESS AT DARTMOUTH COLLEGE, JUNE 9, 2002

Love and compassion are necessities, not luxuries. Without them humanity can not survive.

—TENZIN GYATSO, 14TH DALAI LAMA, DZOGCHEN: HEART ESSENCE OF THE GREAT PERFECTION, 2004

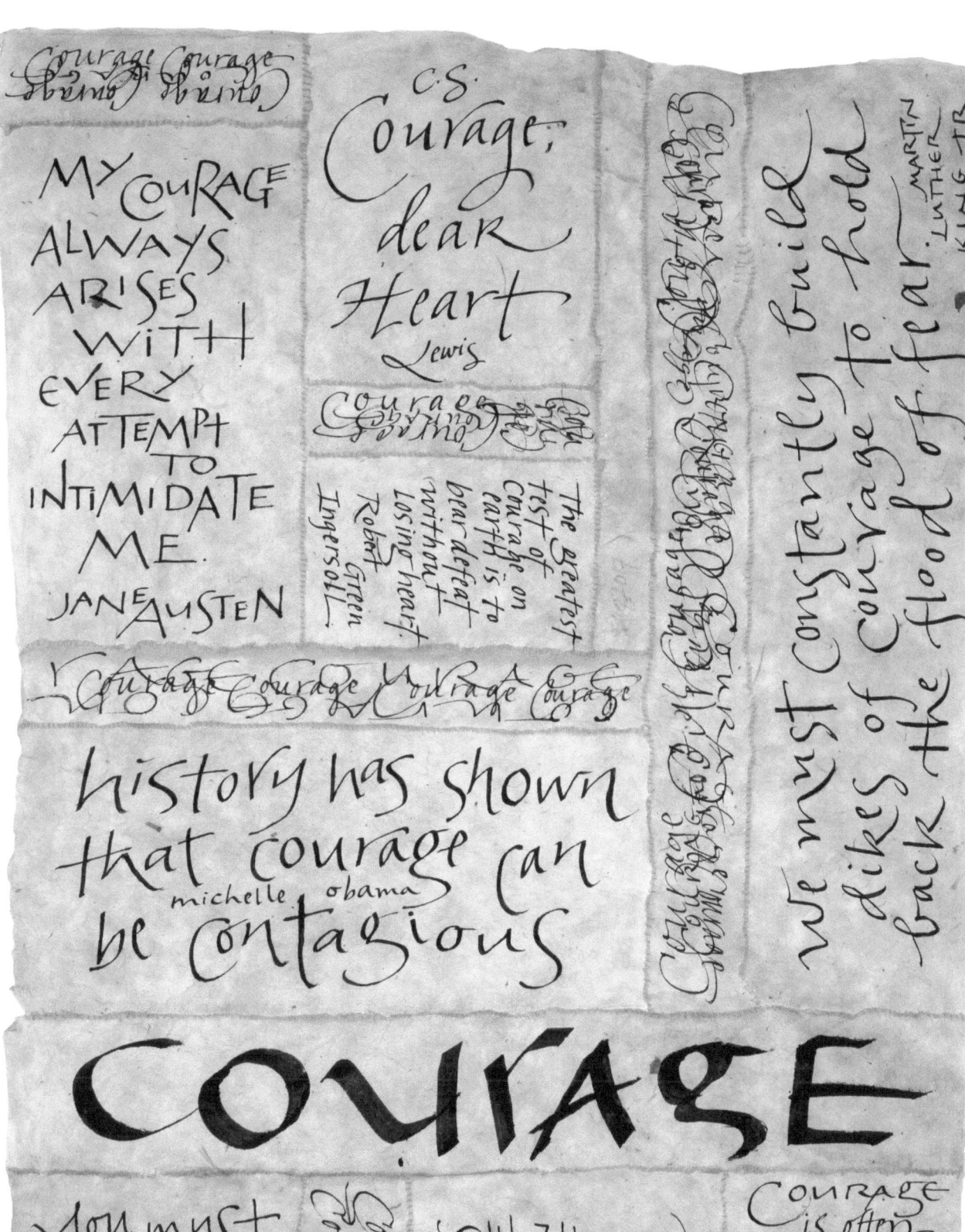

Courage Courage

MY COURAGE ALWAYS ARISES WITH EVERY ATTEMPT TO INTIMIDATE ME. JANE AUSTEN

C.S. Courage, dear Heart Lewis

Courage

The greatest test of Courage on earth is to bear defeat without losing heart. Robert Green Ingersoll

MARTIN LUTHER KING JR

we must constantly build dikes of courage to hold back the flood of fear.

Courage Courage Courage Courage

history has shown that courage can be contagious michelle obama

COURAGE

You must Do the Things You think you cannot Do. ELEANOR ROOSEVELT

Courage Courage

COURAGE IS RESISTANCE TO FEAR MASTERY OF FEAR NOT ABSENCE OF FEAR MARK TWAIN

COURAGE is often FOUND in UNLIKELY places. TOLKIEN

Courage Courage

COURAGE

My courage always arises with every attempt to intimidate me.

—JANE AUSTEN, PRIDE AND PREJUDICE, 1813

Courage, dear heart.

—C. S. LEWIS, VOYAGE OF THE DAWN TREADER, 1952

The greatest test of courage is to bear defeat without losing heart.

—ROBERT GREEN INGERSOLL, THE WORKS OF ROBERT G. INGERSOLL, 1900

... history has shown that courage can be contagious and hope can take on a life of its own.

—MICHELLE OBAMA, KEYNOTE ADDRESS AT THE YOUNG AFRICAN WOMEN LEADERS CONFERENCE, SOWETO, SOUTH AFRICA, JUNE 22, 2011

We must constantly build dikes of courage to hold back the flood of fear.

—MARTIN LUTHER KING, JR., SERMON: ANTIDOTES FOR FEAR, PUBLISHED IN STRENGTH TO LOVE, 1963

You must do the things you think you cannot do.

—ELEANOR ROOSEVELT, YOU LEARN BY LIVING: ELEVEN KEYS FOR A MORE FULFILLING LIFE, 1960

Courage is resistance to fear, mastery of fear, not absence of fear.

—MARK TWAIN, PUDD'NHEAD WILSON'S CALENDAR, 1894

Courage is found in unlikely places.

—J. R. R. TOLKIEN, THE FELLOWSHIP OF THE RING, 1954

COMPASSION AND TOLERANCE ARE NOT A SIGN OF WEAKNESS BUT A SIGN OF STRENGTH.
Tenzin Gyatso, 14th Dalai Lama

What we need in the United States is... love and wisdom, and compassion toward one another, and a feeling of justice toward those who still suffer within our country
Robert F. Kennedy

Compassion Compassion Compassion

Compassion becomes real when we recognize our shared humanity
pema chodron

Until he extends the circle of his compassion to all living things, man will not himself find peace.
Albert Schweitzer

I BELIEVE IN HUMAN DIGNITY AS THE SOURCE OF NATIONAL PURPOSE, IN HUMAN LIBERTY AS THE SOURCE OF NATIONAL ACTION, IN THE HUMAN HEART AS THE SOURCE OF NATIONAL COMPASSION....
JOHN F. KENNEDY

COMPASSION

Compassion is the basis of morality.
ARTHUR SCHOPENHAUER

THE WHOLE IDEA OF COMPASSION IS BASED ON A KEEN AWARENESS OF THE INTERDEPENDENCE OF ALL THESE LIVING BEINGS, WHICH ARE PART OF ONE ANOTHER, AND ALL INVOLVED IN ONE ANOTHER.
THOMAS MERTON

COMPASSION

Compassion and tolerance are not a sign of weakness, but a sign of strength.

—TENZIN GYATSO, 14TH DALAI LAMA, WORDS OF WISDOM: SELECTED QUOTES FROM HIS HOLINESS THE DALAI LAMA, 2004

What we need in the United States is ... love and wisdom, and compassion toward one another, and a feeling of justice toward those who still suffer within our country.

—ROBERT F. KENNEDY, REMARKS ON THE ASSASSINATION OF MARTIN LUTHER KING, JR., INDIANAPOLIS, IN, APRIL 4, 1968

Compassion becomes real when we recognize our shared humanity.

—PEMA CHODRON, THE PLACES THAT SCARE YOU: A GUIDE TO FEARLESSNESS IN DIFFICULT TIMES, 2001

Until he extends the circle of his compassion to all living things, man will not himself find peace.

—ALBERT SCHWEITZER, KULTURPHILOSOPHIE, 1923

I believe in human dignity as the source of national purpose, in human liberty as the source of national action, in the human heart as the source of national compassion ...

—JOHN FITZGERALD KENNEDY, ACCEPTANCE OF THE NEW YORK LIBERAL PARTY NOMINATION FOR PRESIDENT OF THE UNITED STATES, NEW YORK, NY, SEPTEMBER 14, 1960

Compassion is the basis of morality.

—ARTHUR SCHOPENHAUER, ON THE BASIS OF MORALITY, 1840

The whole idea of compassion is based on a keen awareness of the interdependence of all living beings, which are all part of one another, and all involved in one another.

—THOMAS MERTON, ADDRESS DURING CONFERENCE ON EAST-WEST MONASTIC DIALOGUE, BANGKOK, THAILAND, DECEMBER 10, 1968

www.ingramcontent.com/pod-product-compliance
Lightning Source LLC
Chambersburg PA
CBHW050908180526
45159CB00007B/2838